THE FRISIANS

Eric Hoekstra

Xenophobe's Guides

Published by Xenophobe's® Guides.

E-mail: info@xenophobes.com
Web site: www.xenophobes.com

Published 2017

Editor – Catriona Tulloch Scott
Series Editor – Anne Tauté
Cover designer – Vicki Towers
Printer – CPI Antony Rowe, Wiltshire

Cover image – Ice skater at the *Elfstedentocht* Leeuwarden, Friesland, by kind permssion of Micha Klootwijk; www.myimages.nl.

Illustrations – Ice racers ©Alongzo, Cow ©SunshineVector, Cheese ©Wondervendy, Potatoes ©SketchMaster all from Shutterstock; Lighthouse ©Jana Vostal from 123RF.

Acknowledgement is hereby given for the extract from *'wounded continents'*, a poem by Tsjêbbe Hettinga, translated by Susan Massotty and published in *Equinox*, by Friese Pers Boekerij/ Noordboek, 2009.

Print ISBN: 9781906042523
ePub ISBN: 9781908120922
Mobi ISBN: 9781908120953

Contents

Once much larger territorially, Frisia has performed the act of the incredible shrinking man. There are over half a million Frisians, over half a million cows (don't confuse them), 100,000 pigs and 9 million chickens. Another half million (Frisians) emigrated to Amsterdam, Canada, Australia and the USA.

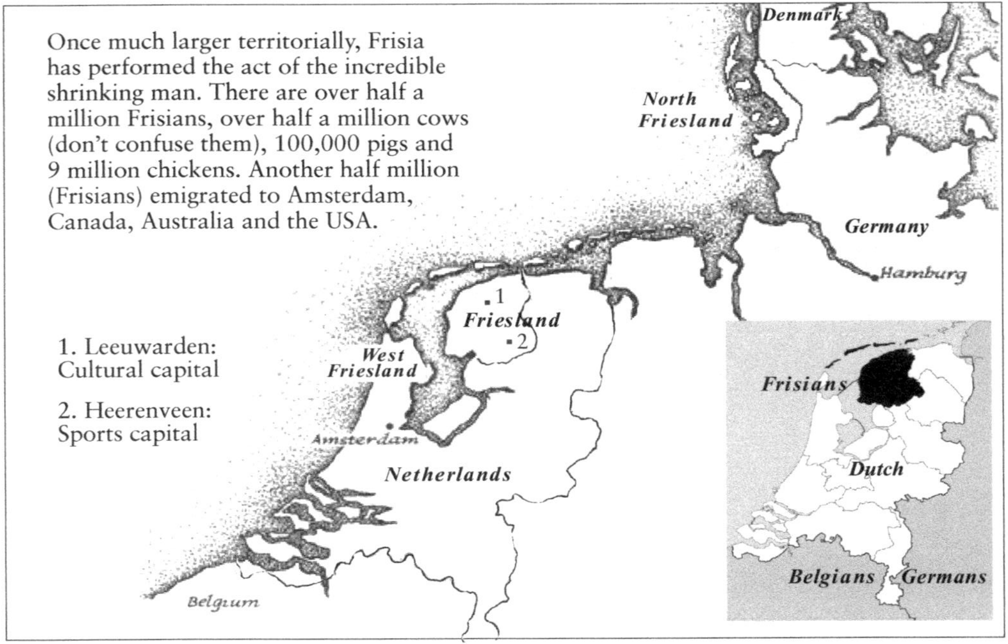

1. Leeuwarden: Cultural capital

2. Heerenveen: Sports capital

Nationalism & Identity

The identity conundrum

Frisia is the English name for a modestly-sized province in The Netherlands which is called Fryslân in the native tongue and Friesland in Dutch. This illustrates the linguistic dilemma of the Frisians: should they speak Frisian or Dutch? Not every Frisian can speak Frisian nowadays, and is a Frisian who cannot speak Frisian a Frisian?

“Not every Frisian can speak Frisian nowadays, and is a Frisian who cannot speak Frisian a Frisian?”

Things do not become any clearer from a study of the map. Foreigners sometimes refer to the Frisians as the West Frisians to distinguish them from their East Frisian cousins in Germany. But the Frisians reserve the name West Frisians for their Dutch Frisian cousins north of Amsterdam, on the other side of lake IJsselmeer. To make matters even more confusing, there are the North Frisians on the islands north of Hamburg. Missing, however, are South Frisians, although some expansive nationalists have begun to refer to the Dutch as such.

Dutch is the official first language of The Netherlands, the nation which Frisians officially belong to. Some of them view this as an unfortunate state of affairs and recently coined the term 'frexit', in support of an exit from The Netherlands, though not the EU. Owing to political agitation the Frisian language has been recognised as the official second language of The Netherlands, but only, of course, in the province of Friesland.

"Frisian has been recognised as the official second language of The Netherlands, but only, of course, in the province of Friesland."

Although Frisian self-respect is inversely proportionate to the province's economic importance, some people cannot help being worried by this (the lack of economic importance, that is, not the exaggerated self-respect). Unemployment causes massive migration to the Rânestêd (Dutch: Randstad), literally 'fringe city', the agglomeration of cities in the western part of The Netherlands, close to the North Sea.

Frisians in search of money and jobs swoop down on Amsterdam, leaving their less brainy cousins to tend the land. Brainlessness does not seem to be hereditary, however, seeing that Frisia continues to produce sons and daughters who are smart enough to move away.

Some Frisian emigrants preserve the countryside myth in the memories of their youth. Having made their fortune, they then return to 'it beste lân fan de ierde' (the world's finest country), as Frisians modestly call their homeland, only to find that cheap houses have taken the place of the trees under which they used to play.

Frisians like to invite others to share their enthusiasm for Frisia. After all, visitors bring in extra cash which keeps the local shopkeepers in business, and tickles Frisian vanity and self-respect. For this reason, if for no other, a strong sense of their own identity is widespread among the natives.

How others regard them

The Frisians successfully withstood Christianisation by violent means for some centuries. As a result they got a very bad press from Frankish propagandists passing themselves off as historians. This may explain their reputation for being heathen barbarians.

“In Frisia, a nobleman could get himself killed just like any ordinary Tom, Dick or Harry.”

Later, when they sturdily withstood Dutch attempts to ‘pacify’ them, they attracted extra attention because they did not take hostages for ransom. Elsewhere this was common practice for captured noblemen. But in Frisia, a nobleman could get himself killed just like any ordinary Tom, Dick or Harry. Naturally, this got them a very bad press from Dutch propagandists passing themselves off as historians.

Nowadays Frisians have a somewhat ambiguous

reputation. On the one hand, they are viewed as arrogant clodhoppers trying to impose the silly language of their ancestors on innocent non-Frisian cohabitants. On the other hand, they earn respect for the tenacity with which they stick to their identity, and for the fact that they have one.

“Relations between the Dutch and the Frisians are never better than during an *elfstedentocht*.”

Whereas the Dutch are cultural magpies, people who cherry-pick from other nations and practise their nationalism in secret, Frisians stick to their own culture and flaunt their love of themselves and their country, which earns them the open jealousy or covert admiration of the Dutch. Their shameless self-admiration is something that aligns the Frisians rather more with the Germans, but that is not something they would be overjoyed to admit.

Relations between the Frisians and the Dutch are never better than during an *alvestêdetocht* (Dutch: *elfstedentocht*), a skating tour along frozen canals that connect eleven cities. Even in a biting northeaster the Dutch come to Frisia as spectators to line the route of this heroic event and cheer the skaters as they glide past.

The Frisians, feeling that

they are finally receiving the appreciation that is due to them, go out of their way to carry coffee and sandwiches to the Dutch supporters FOR FREE. This cannot but amaze the Dutch who are not known to give anything for nothing. The Frisians become for the Dutch the embodiment of what the Dutch themselves once were, before their mercantile spirit took over. After the event, hundreds of letters are sent to the newspapers in which the Dutch express their gratitude for such treatment – letters that are proudly published in the Frisian press. Dutch praise is a rare thing.

“They are tenacious to a degree that often amounts to downright stubborness.”

The Frisians in East Friesland (now German territory) have much the same attraction for the rest of the German nation as the Dutch Frisians have for the Netherlands' Dutch. They appeal as a concept (rather than a people), one that has been thrown overboard as being impractical, and which they would like to forget, but can't.

Which is why it is left to the Frisians to admire themselves.

How they regard themselves

Frisians like to think of themselves as an open-minded, honest, reliable sort of people. They are also stubborn to a degree that often amounts to downright pigheadedness. If circumstances arise in which this is teamed with foolishness, the results are far from ideal. A perfect example of this is the Frisians' refusal in the Middle Ages to build dykes to prevent the land from flooding simply because their neighbours paid less tithes than themselves, or had more land, or did not read the right newspaper.

Instead, to ensure that nobody else would profit from their work they built *terpen*, mounds that stood above the land and were large enough to accommodate villages. Of course, *terpen* won't do if the sea gets rough and the tide is high, so it was their good fortune that during a Spanish invasion in the 16th century, a Spaniard named Caspar de Robles forced them to build dykes. This earned him a statue from later generations – Frisians who were apparently more sensible than their forefathers.

> **“Questioned as to why he had remained standing, Gemma answered: “A Frisian kneels only before God.””**

The Frisians themselves prefer to illustrate their stubbornness with another incident that took place in the 16th century. Philip II of Spain invited all the noblemen to a meeting. When he entered the room, all the noblemen kneeled except one, Gemma van Burmania. Questioned as to why he had remained standing, he answered: “A Frisian kneels only before God." Some may consider this to be a proud answer, or even blatantly arrogant. They would do well to bear in mind that at least Gemma did not require God to kneel before him.

There is little doubt that the Frisians admire themselves. A Dutch reporter asked Franke Sloothaak, the Olympic show jumping champion, if he did not feel that all his aspirations were fulfilled now that he had become the world champion. As was widely reported, the staunch Frisian replied: "Well, you see, I am already a Frisian. That is the highest one can aspire to."

"A people that is so full of itself cannot be expected to spare much thought for others."

How they regard others

Naturally, a people that is so full of itself cannot be expected to spare much thought for others. Nevertheless, the Frisians possess a straightforward evaluation scale by which to judge others: to what extent are they capable of sharing Frisian enthusiasm for Frisia? This will determine to a large extent how those 'others' are regarded by the Frisians.

For example, the Germans are viewed elsewhere in Europe with a degree of disquiet. However, since they come to Frisia to enjoy the winding waterways (not to mention the boats they commission to be built at Frisian boatyards), the attitude towards them can be described as nothing more nor less than benign.

There is an affinity with the Scandinavians, who are also seafaring peoples. The possibility cannot be ignored that the Frisians are basically a Scandinavian tribe. Old Frisian laws have special provisions for crimes committed by Frisians in the service of the Vikings since, having been abducted, they had no choice but to comply with the dastardly deeds of the Norsemen. The punishment for such crimes was much lighter. On the whole, however, the Scandinavians live too far away for the Frisians to hold strong views about them.

“The possibility cannot be ignored that the Frisians are basically a Scandinavian tribe.”

Much less affection is afforded to the Dutch who disregard Frisian culture, refuse to adapt to local customs and exhibit the sort of slick city manners which go against the Frisian grain. Indeed, there is a marked contrast between the interest the Dutch exhibit towards cultural variation outside The Netherlands and the uniformity they expect to exist inside The Netherlands. Alas, this is something the Dutch share with a fair number of Frisians who prefer to be Dutch first, and Frisian last.

Special Relationships

The Frisians consider the Frisians to be the most admirable people on earth. If the name hadn't been nabbed by another nation, they might well have styled themselves 'God's chosen people'.

After being beaten by Emperor Charlemagne in the late 8th century, the Frisians considered themselves to be the Emperor's favourite. Numerous charters survive in which Charlemagne grants special privileges to the Frisians, though few are believed to be genuine.

> **"The Frisians have a special relationship with the Frisians, who they consider to be the most admirable people on earth."**

In summary, the Frisians have a special relationship with themselves and with figures of absolute authority. Like Emperor Charlemagne. As an egalitarian people, this means that when confronted with hierarchy, the Frisians are efficient at dealing with it. Bypassing the middlemen, they address themselves directly to the highest boss, that is, God or the King: after all, they are the only ones they can talk to as equals.

Taxes

It was resistance against taxes that created the Frisian nation. Firstly, the Frisians revolted against the Romans in the year AD 29 because the Roman governor Olennius refused to accept their hides (not their own, but their oxes'): he judged them to be a tad too small to fulfil the terms of the Friso-Roman tax agreement. The Frisians defeated two battalions of cavalry and three battalions of infantry, while 900 Romans were killed in the woods at night, and another 400 committed suicide. Their victory made them famous in the Germanic-speaking world.

Secondly, after their defeat by Charlemagne, the Frisians managed to negotiate special tax privileges: they had to pay tax to the Emperor only, and this gave them a pretext for not paying taxes to any overlord who foolishly imagined he could extract so much as a penny from them. Subsequently, the privilege to levy tax on the Frisians was sold to various parties, each of whom failed to collect it: the Bishop of Utrecht, the Duke of Gelre, the Count of East Frisia, the city of Groningen, various Counts of Holland, and some German Counts. If their descendants were to instigate a claim, the Frisian nation would go broke due to having to pay up several centuries of back taxes.

"If their descendants were to go to court, the Frisian nation would go broke."

Money matters have also unified the Frisian nation in the recent past. This time a fine rather than a tax was involved. A judge with the unfortunate name of 'Hollander' fined two Frisian fishermen because they refused to talk Dutch in court. A journalist criticised the judge for linguistic suppression and was brought to trial. This resulted in a tremendous riot which bears the memorable name of Kneppelfreed, cudgel Friday. It took place in the 1950s when the police's chief method of persuasion was the cudgel.

"Lots of Frisians own a flag and they seize every opportunity to display it."

Kneppelfreed gave the Dutch government such a fright that they immediately turned Frisian into the second official language in the province. Henceforth Frisian could be spoken in court. Now millions in subsidies flow from The Hague to Frisia in order to develop legal terminology in Frisian, to translate law books, and so on. It would have been cheaper to have remitted the original fine.

The flag

The best bit of Frisian culture is its flag. It has immense marketing possibilities. You could even sell *kofjemolke* (Dutch: *koffiemelk*), the creamer that comes in tiny cartons, with such a flag. Which has in fact been done. There used to be a brand of *koffiemelk* called 'Frisian flag'.

Lots of Frisians own a flag and they seize every opportunity to display it. Foolish sociologists conclude from this that Frisians are nationalistic. Ha, if only! No, the real explanation is that Frisians have a keen aesthetic sense. If you own the most beautiful flag in the world, you'd be a fool not to display it. Even the BBC singled it out for attention: they put the shirt of soccer club Heerenveen (which displays the Frisian flag) on a list of ugly soccer shirts.

“The Frisian hearts are love hearts. They stand for Frisian self-love.”

Many non-Frisians wonder about the meaning of the red hearts in the Frisian flag. This is easy to explain. The hearts are love hearts. They stand for Frisian self-love. Foolish historians stubbornly maintain that they stand for the leaves of the yellow water lily. The idea is patently ridiculous, for the leaves of the yellow water lily are green. But since staunch Frisians feel embarrassed to flaunt their love hearts, the historians' explanation has been widely embraced.

Those same historians also maintain that each of the seven hearts represents a so-called Frisian *seelân*, literally sealand, an area defined in some

sense by the sea. These seven sealands are: Westfriesland (north of Amsterdam), Oostergo, Westergo and Zevenwouden (these three make up the province of Frisia), Groningen (adjacent province), Drenthe (adjacent province) and East Friesland (in neighbouring northern Germany). Note again how shallow the lies of the historians are, for it is evident that South Holland and Utrecht would not have been omitted from a real list of Frisian lands.

Character

Enthusiasm

Frisian character oscillates between two extremes: enthusiasm and derision. When enthusiasm is dominant Frisians have a great capacity for exaggeration. Here's an example. An ancient history of the Frisians traced their descent to the army of Alexander the Great in India, but that turned out to be a 19th-century hoax.

“An *elfstedentocht* fires the heroic imagination.”

Here's another example. One of the eleven 'cities' of the *elfstedentocht* has less than 3,000 inhabitants. Enthusiasm is never bigger than during an *elfstedentocht* – an event that fires the heroic imagination. But nearly as important are the preparations. A network of volunteers is set up in order to keep track of the increasing or decreasing thickness of the ice along the route.

Skaters who have been training in Finland return home expecting at least a hypothetical *elfstedentocht*. Usually the skating tour is called off, not because the cities are too small but because the ice is too weak. There have only been 15 since 1908, the last being held in 1997. (Global warming wreaks havoc on age-old customs.)

The chairman of the 'organising committee' reports every day to the press about the chances of the event going ahead. He speaks Dutch with a heavy Frisian accent. Insiders know that his Dutch is flawless when he is not talking to the press.

“Frisians, who have a reputation for surliness, are said to thaw when it freezes.”

When winters do produce enough ice, a city-wide street party takes place in the capital of Leeuwarden on the evening before the race. According to one reporter of the event, 'Frisians, who have a reputation for surliness, are said to thaw when it freezes'. The more so, since the ice is a great matchmaker.

Many a happy couple made their first acquaintance on the skating rink. This is where physical contact is easy and permitted. Girls skating on the rink may be grabbed from behind (at the waist, mind you) and then pushed from one side of the rink to the other, where they regain their liberty. The girl either lets herself be pushed without moving her

limbs herself, or she skates to the boy's rhythm. Couples can also skate in rhythm side by side, the boy's right hand holding the girl's left hand, and the boy's left holding the girl's right. This is a good test for a harmonious marriage. If they don't skate in rhythm, their limbs get entangled and they tumble. Entanglement of limbs has led to many a man's downfall.

The big day itself is extensively covered by the media. People take a day off just to spend 16 hours glued to the television, not just in Frisia but in the whole of The Netherlands. There are camera crews from all over the world. Frisia is finally the centre of the world, if only for a day.

Polarisation

Polarisation is the natural result of exaggeration. The 1920s and 30s had the socialists at one end of the political spectrum, and at the other end the puritans. Each of those groups held about 10% of the votes in the Dutch provinces. The Frisian counterparts each held about 20% of the votes, showing a higher degree of bifurcation than the rest of the country. Frisians polarise.

Polarisation results in a tendency to see things in black and white. This can be very effective when all sorts of fine distinctions merely serve to obfuscate the issue: simplification to get to the heart of the matter is their aim, in the spirit of Churchill rather than Chamberlain (at least in theory). Hence it cannot be accidental that it was a Frisian premier, Pieter Gerbrandy, who guided The Netherlands through the Second World War. That was the only occasion that the country had a Frisian premier. When the going gets really tough, the Dutch need a Frisian.

> **"When the going gets really tough, the Dutch need a Frisian."**

The medieval battle-cry ran: '*leaver dea as slaaf*' ('better dead than enslaved', or 'live free or die') – an obvious case of exaggeration, especially since Frisians do not object to being a *leanslaaf* (a paid slave). It might be objected that battle-cries always polarise, the more so when they are medieval. True, but what other people would still display the slogan on their house-front today?

The slogan can be found even on the North Frisian isles off the German coast, close to the Danish border. The North Frisian language is incomprehensible to the ears of their Dutch Frisian cousins, but the sentiments of the battle-cry remain the same.

Crisis management

The Frisians are good at crisis management for it is then that they work miracles.

In 1452, the Dutch tried to invade Frisia. A large fleet landed in the south-west tip of the province. The Dutch nobility started to reconnoitre, separating themselves from the rest of the invasion army. A farmer spying on them noticed this and, alerting his comrades, an attack was mounted when the knights were riding slowly through a muddy meadow. The knights in their armour were pulled down with ropes from their horses which could not gain speed on the muddy soil – and killed. Frisian nationalists began commemorating this event in the 1950s; a bit on the late side, one might be inclined to think.

“The Frisians are good at crisis management for it is then that they work miracles.”

Also in the 1950s the Frisian soccer club Heerenveen was playing Ajax Amsterdam (the premier league Dutch team). After 45 minutes Ajax led by 5-1. But the Frisians rolled up their sleeves and won 6-5. Whereas others might forget such events within a decade or so, the Frisians cherish them, adding them to the stock of anecdotes that they like to tell about themselves to themselves.

How many other people would have made that soccer match the subject of an outdoor spectacular, presented in the very same stadium as their win? A mixture of media, art and outdoor play, the show revolved around the life of the legendary Frisian soccer player Abe Lenstra. Johan Cruijff (the Dutch Maradona) used to pale in sunny Spain upon hearing Abe's name. The spectacle even included the landing of a helicopter on the playing field. It seems that the organisers are still in debt, but never mind about that. Like the victorious event on which it was based, the show was a worthy Frisian feat, capable of drawing tears of admiration from even the most anti-nationalist spectator.

“They spurn superiority that is the result of hard work. It must be seen to be playful and effortless.”

Of course, the purpose of such stories is to bolster the view the Frisians entertain about themselves as being top of the world if they have a mind to be. Furthermore, unlike the Germans, they spurn superiority that is the result of hard work. It must be seen to be playful and effortless. To be truly valuable, the feat must be rare. This is generally not a problem: Heerenveen, for example, rarely manages to win against Ajax.

Teasing

Loving tenderness is not an emotion that is avidly exhibited in Frisia, not even among family members. To find an outlet, their emotion is diverted and shows up as a tendency towards teasing, since that which is contrary is the closest you can get to the thing itself, if the thing itself is forbidden.

A consequence of this tendency was that in the past it was customary for the friends of a recently married couple to play a joke on them. On arriving home the newly-weds could expect to find the legs of their bed sawn off, a bath tap turned on or the house covered in dust sheets – long before artists like Christo starting wrapping up bridges and other buildings. And these were only a few of the more innocent pranks.

Surliness

Frisians are often considered surly and unapproachable. It's a trait they share with many countries whose northern inhabitants are thought to be more serious than their southern equivalents. A travelling salesman recalls entering a Frisian company canteen. Salesmen tend to be jovial so he greeted everybody with a smile and much friendly waving of the hands and noddings of the head in all directions, saying:

"A good day to you, gentlemen!"

To which one of them replied:

"Mind your own business. We decide for ourselves whether this day will be good or not."

Naturally, this happened in the northern part of Frisia.

Derision

Derision is useful to keep enthusiasm in check, an exuberance that might otherwise lead to foolishness. Derision, scepticism and cynicism are all indicative of the darker side of Frisian nature. Here we must look to find the causes of the alleged high degree of suicides among Frisians as compared to the rest of the country. It fits, though, with the Frisian tendency towards polarisation: everything or nothing. It is usually nothing. Or as the most popular urban proverb has it, well-known in Leeuwarden (Ljouwert in Frisian):

“Anyone in authority is the immediate butt of Frisian disapprobation.”

‘*Ut is niks, ut was niks en ut sal oek nooit wat wurde.*’ (It is nothing, it was nothing and it never will be anything).

All growlers and grumblers cherishing this proverb were unpleasantly surprised when Leeuwarden was nominated Cultural Capital of Europe 2018.

It can safely be assumed that it is the tendency towards derision that is responsible for the egalitarian nature of the Frisians. Anyone in authority is the immediate butt of their disapprobation in the form of mockery and derision. Strangely enough, journalists and doctors seem to have acquired authority without being ridiculed: a sure sign of decadence in the Frisian tribe.

Conversation

Frisian conversation freely delves into the personal domain so as to satisfy the questioner's curiosity. Foreigners are asked what they have for breakfast, why they wear the clothes they are wearing and why they came here: no offence intended.

Opinions are aired about all sorts of subjects, and the last thing required is knowledge. This is due to the influence of the newspapers which have inculcated the Frisian nation for two centuries with the importance of 'having an opinion'. Hence there are lots of Frisians walking around publicly displaying their ignorance and getting away with it. This ignorance is not compensated for by any special respect for experts, such as the Germans or the French have. The only thing required for having an opinion is a daily reading of the newspaper.

“Opinions are aired about all sorts of subjects and the last thing required is knowledge.”

If visitors want to shock Frisians, they should say they don't read newspapers. Frisians swill think the outsiders are pulling their leg. This especially applies to older Frisians. Youngsters apply to the Internet for their opinions.

Among family members, conversation may take the form of nagging or niggling or it may take the form of spirited verbal sparring in which each tries to uncover and exaggerate the faults of the other, real or imaginary. This is either deadly earnest or playfully comedic, depending on the psychology of the family involved.

Strangers will not see this for Frisians only practise this sport in the seclusion of the family circle. It was probably invented as a way of getting through long dreary winters, when each family led an isolated existence on its *terp*.

“Spirited verbal sparring tries to uncover and exaggerate the faults of the other, real or imaginary.”

Of course, there were the Holstein-Friesians, but their contribution to conversation was negligible for they are not neighbours, but cows. Besides, the Holstein-Friesians came from East Friesland in northern Germany, so they would speak a different language anyway because the Netherlands' Frisian and Germany's Frisian are not mutually intelligible. For people that is; for cows it may be different.

A favourite topic of conversation is the weather, but this is not used as an excuse for grumbling. Frisians like all sorts of weather. A little rain is good for the garden. A little sun is good for the crops. They only complain if there is a drought or a deluge, because that is not good for either. As for cold and frost, that makes for healthy weather, and besides, an *elfstedentocht* may be in the offing. It is probably their farmer's instinct which makes them appreciate various sorts of weather, realising that changeable weather is part and parcel of getting the most out of nature.

The topic of the weather is closely associated with the look of the garden and with the view. Natural sequences of remarks run like this: "It's sunny, the air feels fresh, the petunias are flowering, the tomatoes are coming on well", not all of these together, of course. Or: "Come outside, the mists are rising, there's a beautiful sunset."

"The Frisians have a highly developed aesthetic appreciation of the beauty of their landscapes."

Descending from farmers, the Frisians have a highly developed aesthetic appreciation of the beauty of their landscapes, even if their taste in Ming china leaves something to be desired. Dozens of picture books are churned out every year, glorifying the Frisian landscape. Many painters have adopted the Frisian landscape as their muse.

It has to be admitted that Frisian landscapes are many and varied: huge skies, stretches of wet sand that appear when the tide runs out, lakes and sailing boats, meadows sprinkled with trees, woods sprinkled with meadows, sea sprinkled with islands, islands sprinkled with inlets, and picturesque towns and villages. Small wonder then that tourism is Frisia's main asset.

Behaviour

The boss in the family

In the Frisian family the man is the boss, women take second place, children third, while for grandparents there is no place. The famous Frisian novel *The ten children of Afke* shows the division as follows: the husband gets meat and potatoes, the mother and the children get potato peelings and skimmed milk.

The number of working women is lower in Frisia (and the rest of The Netherlands) than in most other countries of the EU. Furthermore, working women tend to be employed in what are deemed to be 'womanly' professions, such as hospital nurses. If women are found at all in, say, an institute of mathematics, then it is not as a professor but as a professor's secretary. No doubt this is linked to the dominance of the male in arduous agrarian conditions, and its accompanying need for a lack of sentimentality that characterises Frisian society.

The elderly

This is no country for old men, nor for old women. Individualism and independence form the Frisian ideal, but how can you be independent if you are too old to mow the grass or buy your own television guide?

Frisian efficiency has come up with the same solution as rival Germanic tribes – the old people's home. Mediterranean countries opt for this solution only for those unfortunate enough to be without family. Well, no old Frisian, it appears, has family.

Having one's parents in the house is usually seen as a big problem, or a sign of asocial behaviour, or a serious breach of the ideal of independence. Grown-up children would not want to live with their parents, nor parents with their children. Strangely enough, dependence upon the state, as implied by paying taxes or by living in state-subsidised old people's homes, is not felt by the elderly to be a breach of the independence ideal: the principle solely applies to family.

“Having one's parents in the house is usually seen as a sign of asocial behaviour or as a serious breach of the ideal of independence.”

The layout of the type of houses that are common do not allow for peaceful co-existence between more than one couple either: one bathroom, one kitchen, one living-room. Such small houses have been purposely built to render the Mediterranean solution impossible.

Social responsibility often replaces the lack of

family affection. Old people's homes and hospitals employ volunteers to visit residents and patients if their family does not show up at visiting hours.

With an increasingly ageing population and less funding being available for welfare, the number of old folk's homes is being cut back, so a new policy has come into being. The elderly are encouraged to live as long as possible in their own homes. It is financially less costly to be a single member household than a two member household. Lots of older people constitute single households. Here's a ready market for internet dating – if only the government wouldn't impose higher taxes on those who start living together.

"The elderly are encouraged to live as long as possible in their own homes."

Children and pets

The Frisian ideal of independence as applied to family similarly results in a negative valuation of children. But how can you be independent if you are too young to mow the grass or to buy your own television guide?

Children are appreciated to the extent that they are independent, that is inactive – that is sleeping and not asking for a glass of water.

This behaviour backfires when the children are

growing up. Generational conflicts begin with skirmishes to do with criticism, which may drag on for years until they happily end with the children leaving the house or being kicked out of it.

Pets, in contrast, get far more favourable treatment. To begin with they are much more independent. They don't criticise you, they never say you are wrong, they poo in other people's gardens and they don't sue you for your inheritance.

> **"Pets get far more favourable treatment than children. They don't criticise you."**

Pets, but not children, are allowed to beg for food, to ask for attention and to sleep on beds other than their own. Nobody complains if your pet has fleas, but if your child has fleas, an angry school doctor comes to visit you.

Of course, all this is slightly exaggerated; the school doctor will not necessarily be angry if your child has fleas.

Eccentric behaviour

Eccentric behaviour is less tolerated in cities than in villages. Villagers consider it amusing. Townspeople, perhaps wiser than their village cousins, consider it threatening.

Absolute uniformity reigns at work, although an exception was made for a researcher to take his dog to his office. Unsurprisingly, this case of eccentric behaviour concerns pets, who are valued more than people. There's even a case of a refugee who couldn't make an impression on an immigration official by saying that his family had been murdered by the Iraqi dictator Saddam Hussein. Then the refugee noticed the dog by the official's side, and added that they also murdered dogs – which instantly earned him a passport.

“There appears to be a bleak nihilist streak running across the Frisian psyche.”

All this makes perfect sense, for Frisian culture has always strongly relied on farmers. And they always go to work accompanied by the animals they love. Or sell. Or eat.

Manners

Frisians tend to lack decorum and to view politeness as imperiousness. Thus many Frisians hesitate to enter a superior shop (coffee shop or otherwise), not because it would be more expensive but rather because the luxurious surroundings would make them feel ill at ease.

There appears to be a bleak nihilist streak running through the Frisian psyche: nothing is sacred. Frisians only suppress the tendency to act in accordance with this trait in order to make social contact possible. Social contact turns them into actors playing the role of civilised persons (all of which supports the hypothesis that the Frisians really descend from the Vikings).

In Frisia social niceties are not placed high on the agenda. On trains you are allowed to put your feet on the seat opposite you, even if there is somebody sitting on the one adjacent to it. However, official train regulations do dictate that you should either remove your shoes or put a newspaper on the seat on which you rest your feet. Should your fellow traveller remove his shoes, you must pray he changes his socks daily.

"In Frisia, social niceties are not placed high on the agenda."

A Frisian family is a collection of outspoken barbarians, rather than an entity in which people express mutual respect for each other. It is not only common to judge, ridicule or make fun of everybody you know when they are not present, but close family members can be ridiculed while they are present, though to be fair, this sort of behaviour is only displayed in the intimacy of the family circle, not when there are visitors or strangers present. These last are treated better than brothers, sisters or parents (and grown-up children visiting their parents are expected to make polite conversation with whomsoever is also visiting).

If visitors arrive at dinner time without arranging

to do so, the normal thing to do is to apologise for the fact that there is not enough food to invite them to dinner and wait for them to push off. The alternative is to invite them to dinner: but it's an invitation visitors are expected to refuse since everybody knows that it cannot be in earnest. Coffee should always be offered – whatever else isn't – although there are cases on record of indignant mothers not offering coffee to their visiting daughters because they arrived without notice.

“Alternation between enthusiasm and despondency seems to be stronger in Frisians than in surrounding nations.”

It is not unusual to be very friendly with the neighbours. Before you know it, they come uninvited on your birthday. Social play-acting is so strongly embedded that it is nearly impossible to refuse your neighbours anything, however easy it may be to refuse your family everything. Mediterranean peoples are ruled by their families. Frisians are ruled by their neighbours.

Gestures

The Frisians don't have much in the way of facial gestures. But when they become enthusiastic (that is, when they start exaggerating), their eyes continually flick from side to side, as if they are taking grain from a barn and throwing it out. Their intonation, never flat anyway, takes on a sing-song quality that is reminiscent of the Swedes. They may gesture wildly to illustrate their point, laugh a lot and be quite charming. On the other hand, when they are morose, grumpy or gloomy they do not gesture at all. Alternation between enthusiasm and despondency, good humour or surliness, seems to be stronger in Frisians than in surrounding nations.

Where did they develop this artistic temperament? When, on their *terpen*, they were cut off from each other in cloudy, wet winters brooding over their thoughts? The Frisian humour probably just reflects the extreme conditions of the weather, which either corresponds to joyful frugality or to sombre monotony.

Attitudes and Values

Moderation

It is understandable that a people given to exaggeration should have for its chief ideal moderation. It is a mode generally achieved as long as it concerns things that are not thought to be vitally important. This applies to the vast majority of matters.

The principle of moderation gives Frisians an excuse for being satisfied with mediocrity: average efforts, average attainments, average results, all are seen as a reflection of wise moderation. They believe that they could make their superiority obvious if only they had a mind to do so. But they haven't. The ideals of moderation and wisdom act as a cover for lethargy and self-gratification.

> **"Frisians are the ultimate Taoists, practising 'action through non-action'."**

This results in a situation where you find bus-drivers who have built the best amateur telescopes in The Netherlands, elementary school teachers who can outwit university professors, postmen with university degrees, and so on.

Frisians are the ultimate Taoists, practising 'action through non-action'. A flash of self-knowledge has given the following proverb to the nation: 'A Frisian only walks as far as you kick him.'

Freedom and independence

The individual Frisian is more independent than, say, the individual Chinese. A small nation cannot but prize freedom and independence.

But collectively the Frisians have failed to produce the ultimate in collective independence – the state – probably due to their innate inertia and belief in their effortless superiority.

The hard-working Dutch, by contrast, produced a state. But Frisians will say that this is only because they were after tax money from their citizens.

When the Frisians joined the Dutch state, they may have been thinking: let's pay those taxes as long as we're not bothered by the bureaucracy. This hope was soon squashed. What may also have helped the Frisians to make up their minds about joining The Netherlands was the fact that Spanish armies stood lined up along their borders.

Class

Whereas the Dutch descend spiritually from preachers and merchants, and the Germans from military men and civil servants, the Frisians have been moulded by generations of farmers and school teachers. The ruling class used to consist nearly exclusively of farmers. This explains many properties of the Frisians, their appreciation of the beauty of nature and their understanding of the necessity of living in harmony with it. All Frisian intellectuals descend from farmers, either in the first degree or in the second. It is usually the farmers who are the first to experiment with new machinery or new methods of farming, often inventing them themselves. It is the farmers who reinstated Frisian as a language, by reading and writing it.

“The Frisians have been moulded by generations of farmers and school teachers.”

Religion and politics

The Frisian Menno Simons created a form of protestantism in Frisia at the same time as Luther and Calvin came to the fore. His gentle brand attracted followers in the northern Netherlands and northern Germany. Due to persecution, the Mennonites fled to Russia, Canada, America and Mexico, where they can still be found, living in harmony with nature long before the word 'green' took on its current political overtones.

"Frisian aggression made an exception for Menno Simons, but this should not be held against them."

Mennonite gentleness could never have become much of a success in the aggressive climate of Germanic Europe. Frisian aggression made an exception for Menno Simons, but this should not be held against them.

The puritans have held power, politically, morally and spiritually since the 17th century when The Netherlands won the war of independence against Spain and kicked out Catholicism. It wasn't until the 1960s that the socialists got the upper hand (politically, morally, and so on). Nowadays, socialism is on the wane, and populism on the rise.

The struggle between puritans

and socialists lives on in Frisian literature produced by the older generation. Whenever a puritan appears in the books of Rink van der Velde (No.1 best-selling author), you may be sure he is going to pull a dirty trick on the novel's main character. Frisian puritans (according to van der Velde) hypothesize as follows: 'What the heck, all the non-puritans will go to hell, so why bother treating them well if the Boss is going to scourge them anyway?'

"Whenever a puritan appears in the books of van der Velde, you may be sure he's going to pull a dirty trick on the novel's main character."

Simke Kloosterman, on the other hand, a writer and proud farmer's daughter, held the socialists responsible for social unrest and civil insubordination. She was wealthy.

Many talented Frisians were prevented from exploiting their natural talents simply because they were born into the wrong class (the class of the poor), and took up the only career that offered some prospect of power and promotion: politics. Those black-and-white days may be over now that the socialists have become the new elite, but the Frisians, with their preference for black and white, still glorify them in their literature. This is why it is said that in Frisia things happen 50 years later than elsewhere in the world.

Individualism

The Frisians have never conformed to standard ideas of behaviour: neither in terms of adhering to rules (as the Germans do) or following unwritten rules (the Dutch), or even breaking the rules (the Italians). The nihilist streak in them makes them dismissive of whatever does not suit them individually.

> **"The Frisians have never conformed to standard ideas of behaviour."**

Given their individualism, one would never expect them to be keen on societies. Yet they are. There are all sorts of societies in Frisia, even in the smallest villages. Whatever these concern – sports, charity, the theatre, politics, religion – within them people are purposeful and well organised.

Throughout history, the Frisians have been anarchic and disorganised. The people never managed to form a political unity. But a weakness is also a strength. The lack of political unity proved a tremendously effective defence against foreign invaders. Whoever tried to gain power inside Frisia was soon bogged down in the mire of unreliable and unpredictable political factions. If the metaphorical bogs were not sufficient, there were always the real bogs to take care of unwanted foreigners. It was not until 1500, when most bogs had been drained, that the duke of Saxony managed to unify the province.

All this goes to show that the Frisians are strong-willed at the individual level. This fits perfectly with the fact that their dominant emotion is self-admiration. Perhaps they are the first post-modernists, since they have no ambition other than doing what they want to do and trying to establish what it is they want to do. The latter takes up so much of their time that they are in danger of not managing to do the former.

“Frisian wives are obsessed with cleanliness.”

The lack of a collective goal has a positive consequence: nowhere else is it possible to encounter such a large variety of psychological types unhampered in their (possibly pathological) development. What they do have in common though, is their determination to defend the right to be what they want to be, whatever that may be.

Obsessions

A clean house

Frisian wives are obsessed with cleanliness, not so much personal cleanliness as cleanliness of the house. It may be their menfolk who are responsible for this. If your man has been standing in cow dung all day, you would be quite keen to keep it outside. Besides, if you want to make butter and cheese it is necessary that everything is spotlessly clean: the least bacteria may ruin your product and leave you without food all winter long.

So, the garden looks cared for, the house is freshly painted and the kitchen is spic-and-span. The owner's armpits may never have seen a deodorant in their life but the house floors are washed more often than those who step on them.

Nature first

In keeping with their farming and close-to-nature background, the Frisians believe in 'naturalness'. They are a people who have cohabited with cows and horses for more than 2,000 years. In earlier times, their houses were constructed like barns, with stalls at one end. Sharing one large space kept humans and animals warm in the bitter winters. People used to wash once a month in a tub of cold water. With the advent of running water, the body wash process was sped up to once a week. But Frisians have not entirely been won over by the new-fangled fondness for taking a shower every day as happens in American movies. Besides, water is not for free.

“The Frisians believe in naturalness. They have cohabited with cows and horses for more than 2,000 years.”

Frisians take a commonsensical approach to hygiene. A couple stayed overnight in the house of some acquaintances. In the morning the female guest assured her host that it was not necessary to change the bed-clothes since 'they had not had sex'.

Frisians are not lovers of French perfume or aftershave. It is the smell of freshly mown grass that enchants them, or their own smell while they are mowing. Being used to the pong of cow dung from an early age, they do not turn up their noses at it. Rather, cow dung is a symbol of fertility, a symbol of the cyclic exchange between nature and man. And the smell of it raises memories of youth and happiness.

"Being used to the pong of cow dung from an early age, they do not turn up their noses at it."

This world view leaves little room for taboos about body parts or functions, a fact which is reflected in the language. In the words of one saying: 'Give away your ass and shit through your ribs.' It's an injunction to look after one's own interests.

The instinct for cleanliness is on the wane: external surfaces of hospital windows are washed more often than the very floors internally. This is dictated by the principle of social relevance: the windows, but not the floors, can be viewed from the outside.

Systems

Aggression, crime and punishment

Frisians prefer the sort of law and order that is favoured among quiet anarchists. Ideally, they would prefer for there to be no laws, with everybody minding his or her own business. They still believe in their heart of hearts that this is possible.

> **"Ideally, they would prefer for there to be no laws, with everybody minding his or her own business."**

Since countries with heavy punishments tend to have more crime than countries with light punishments, punishments for crimes are light – although this may, on occasion, offend the victim's sense of justice.

It seems as if the Frisians do not make the modern distinction between verbal and physical aggression. In one of his bestsellers the Dutch author Frederik Hermans makes a point of this. He writes: *'Somebody yelled "Let's give him a sound beating"; he was a Frisian of course.'*

Education

The two oldest universities of The Netherlands are Leiden in Holland, and Franeker in Frisia.

Unfortunately, Franeker was shut down by Napoleon, and the Dutch did not bother to reopen it after Waterloo. To make up for this, the Dutch government participated financially in the founding of the Frisian Academy, an institute for the study of Frisian culture and history.

Frisian is an optional subject in secondary school, but it does not get much respect from school boards. The secondary school which the author attended even has a Saxon name, Sevenwolden, just to spite the Frisians, who would have preferred the mellow flow of the word Sânwâlden, Seven Woods. So Frisian is as non-existent in secondary school as the local forests which have all but been cut down.

“Frisian is an optional subject in secondary school but it does not get much respect from school boards.”

Two hours of Frisian are obligatorily given in primary school. Those who fail to acquire it there are obliged to study it in the University of Groningen or the University of Amsterdam and in various universities in Germany.

Frisians cannot blame the Dutch government for the fact that there is more Frisian in German universities than in Dutch ones. Recently, the Dutch minister of education proposed giving all university classes in English instead of in Dutch. If the Dutch don't even care about their own language, how can they be expected to care about the Frisian language? It seems at times that Frisians bother as little about their language as the Dutch.

Happily, Frisian is on the rise with young people on social media, especially in the intimacy of WhatsApp.

Bureaucracy

Possibly in recognition of the unruly nature of its people, red tape rules supreme in Frisia. Take housing. Every little change a house-owner wants to make to his home is disallowed unless he has applied for and received a permit for it: whether it be an extra window, an extra room or (in the case of a building of national importance) an acceptable door knocker.

"Possibly in recognition of the unruly nature of its people, red tape rules supreme in Frisia."

It can take several months before you finally hear that your request has been turned down. Most Frisians therefore don't bother to apply. If they are questioned by the authorities on some building irregularity, they can usually get away with saying that the change was made by the previous owner.

There are committees judging designs for new houses, ironically called Beauty Committees. They veto anything out of the ordinary, unless the applicant is an architect, in which case anything but the ordinary is permitted. Interestingly, the architect usually happens to be a member of the Beauty

Committee. The government proposed a plan to rein in the powers of the Beauty Committees, but this plan was only put into effect in a version sufficiently watered down so as to leave everything unchanged.

Conceptual architecture has given Friesland many ugly buildings along with beautiful explanations of why they fit in with the landscape or local history. For example, a grey slab of a building turns out to be a reference to grey slabs of turf that used to be dug from there in the past. Spin doctors can learn much from these Frisians.

Transport

Transport is efficient and expensive. A network of buses used to connect all the little villages to each other and to the towns and an overwhelming majority of the Frisians is in favour of maintaining what remains of these little bus routes. However, they all own cars and many an empty bus can be seen riding through the meadows.

“The larger towns may boast of having a train station. Sometimes trains even stop there.”

The larger towns may boast of having a train station. Sometimes trains even stop there. Nowadays there is pressure to commercialise the state-owned railway lines, especially the ones that are not profitable. The latter include all lines in Frisia, which is less densely populated than the rest of The Netherlands. It is not possible to predict whether this will ultimately have a good or bad effect. However, Frisians know that one thing must be impossible, which is that train-tickets become even more expensive than they already are.

> **"Frisians enjoy drama. It fits with their natural inclination for exaggeration."**

Frisia used to be connected to Amsterdam by boat. The boat would depart in the morning and return late at night. There is many a story about Frisian merchantmen going on the morning boat, getting drunk in Amsterdam, sleeping it off on the boat home, and waking to find themselves back in Amsterdam again.

Leisure & Pleasure

The theatre

Frisians enjoy drama. It fits with their natural inclination for exaggeration. After all, actors on a stage show things not as they are but magnified so that everybody can understand what is going on.

Waling Dijkstra, a 19th-century baker and writer, took to the stage in order to spread the use of the Frisian language. He and his friend, Tjibbe van der Meulen, visited Frisian villages to perform sketches, tell jokes and enact comical scenes.

For most people attending their performances it was the first time they heard Frisian spoken in public instead of just within the family circle. It often happened that a farmer would come to shake hands with them afterwards, with tears in his eyes, saying: "I did not know our language was so beautiful." It was an overwhelming experience for them to hear the language of those they were closest to suddenly being used for comedy and drama.

Nowadays even the smallest village may have a drama society. Its members practise in a real theatre or in a place used for the purpose such as a pub or a school. Hence a relatively large number of famous Dutch actors is actually Frisian or of Frisian descent, and some of the best movies have been made by Frisian directors. For instance, Pieter Verhoeff's colourful view of the 1950s in *De fjoertoer* (*The lighthouse*).

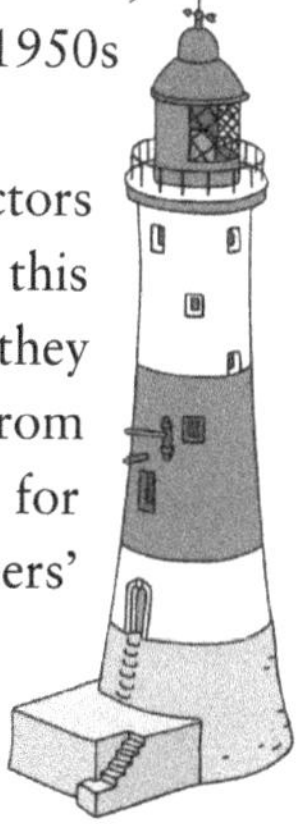

In real life, the Frisians behave as actors only when they get excited. How often this happens depends on the region of Frisia they hail from. The 'Klaikers' or clayfolk from the northern part have a reputation for being cold-blooded, whereas the 'Wâldsjers' or woodfolk from the southern part represent the Frisian version of the Mediterranean temperament. Perfect poise and balance is only encountered in the 'Súdwesthoeke' or the South-West, the region which produced the modest author of this text.

Sports

Frisians, who are easily bogged down by the monotony of daily life, flourish when they can skate in a crystal-white landscape under a blue winter sky. Everybody is in good humour, their aesthetic sense is sharpened, and there is a tremendous feeling of harmony between people and nature.

Skating, the Frisians' national sport, was exported from Frisia to the rest of the world. Archaeologists have found bones, carved in the form of skates, with holes in them for foot bindings – evidence that dates back to Roman times. Skating is such a pleasure that villagers all over Frisia will flood a fallow field to provide a rink for winter fun.

“Frisians flourish when they can skate in a crystal-white landscape under a blue winter sky.”

Foreigners should not be fooled by the newspapers. Whenever the press talks of a Dutch skating champion, whether it be the Olympic Games or the World Championships, you can be sure it is a Frisian. It is no accident that the names of gold-medal winners like Zandstra, Ritsma, Postma all end in '-a'. All names ending in -stra or -ma are exclusively Frisian.

When Frisia got a new governor called Wiegel, he was soon affectionately referred to as Wiegelsma.

Two other popular sports are *fierljeppen* and *kaatsen*. *Kaatsen*, a game similar to American handball, is played with an incredibly hard ball. The game is so frustrating that many players start kicking the ball out of annoyance, and that was how soccer was born.

Fierljeppen, in contrast, is a noble sport. The *fierljepper* uses a light wooden pole seven metres long in order to vault a canal. This is how it goes. The *fierljepper* runs with the pole, hurls it like a javelin into the water, and leaps onto it. His weight forces the pole to bend and he monkey-climbs it higher and higher so that it will arc over to the other side. For the audience it is ace entertainment with a three-way outcome. One, everything goes well – a worthy victory. Two, as he climbs, the athlete throws the pole off balance so that he and the pole topple sidelong into the water. Three, the pole's movement is choked by canal mud and the athlete, like a flag that is being lowered, begins his ignominious downward slide into the water.

“Whenever the press talks of a Dutch skating champion, you can be sure it is a Frisian.”

Another uniquely Frisian delight is *wadlopen* (in Frisian, *waadrinne*), walking the *wad* – a vast expanse of peanut butter-coloured mud and sand exposed by the receding tide – which lies between the Frisian mainland and the Frisian isles. This area, including the isles, is called the Wadden. *Wadlopers* (*wad* walkers) are those intrepid souls who squelch their way across this stretch of sucking sands.

Though guided by an expert who knows his way around, it is difficult and exhausting and not without risk. Wad walkers sometimes have to make large detours before arriving at a place where they can cross a tidal channel, often sinking to their thighs in the mud while doing so. People in other countries pay good money at spas for this kind of thing.

“A uniquely Frisian delight is walking the *wad* – a vast expanse of peanut butter-coloured mud and sand.”

Drinking & Eating

According to Frisians, the Dutch national drink *jenever*, Dutch gin, is a tasteless, colourless thing, characteristic of the Dutch psyche. In contrast, the Frisians' national drink is a tasty, ruby-red liqueur called Beerenburg. It is 30% alcohol and contains many herbs such as licorice, sandalwood, gentian root, bay leaf – some of them medicinal to keep up appearances. Unlike German Jägermeister, French

Cointreau or Scottish Drambuie it is not sweet. This makes Beerenburg a curious favourite because Frisians have a very sweet tooth.

Evil tongues claim Beerenburg to be of Amsterdam origin, but they fail to take into account the origin of the Amsterdam inventor, who must have been a Frisian. After all, many people migrated in the past from Frisia to seek their fortune in wealthy Amsterdam. Whatever the case, the major Beerenburg brands are based in Frisia.

“Beerenburg is a curious favourite because Frisians have a very sweet tooth.”

The average Frisian drinks his coffee with 0.67 more spoons of sugar than the average Dutchman, and with 0.81 more spoons of sugar than the average German. This only goes to prove that the average Frisian spoon is smaller than either its Dutch or German counterparts.

Milk and cheese

For over two millennia the Frisians have enjoyed cows' milk and products derived from it like cheese, butter, cream and buttermilk.

For a time there was a popular advertisement for milk featuring a little Frisian boy who recommended three glasses of milk if you wanted to grow. If that little boy was right, it explains why the

Frisians, with their tremendous milk consumption, are so tall. Indeed, Dante described one of the giants in the centre of hell as follows: *'If you put three Frisians on top of each other, you don't even reach the giant's belly button.'*

Not much has changed since his time: Frisians are still tall. Another account explains their height as a survival trait developed after centuries of inundation: only the tallest could keep their heads above water.

“Frisian cheese looks smooth like a young girl and is a happy yellow.”

Frisian cheese is exported all over the world. A jealous French minister of export once exclaimed, after the sales figures for French cheese had fallen again: “Look at the Frisians! They manage to sell a tasteless cheese all over the world!” Frisians know why. French cheese is smelly, Frisian cheese smells nice. French cheese is sticky, Frisian cheese is not. French cheese looks wrinkled like an old hag, Frisian cheese looks smooth like a young girl. French cheese is sickly pale, Frisian cheese is a happy yellow. That is why Frisian cheese guarantees high sales, as any marketeer can tell you. Predictably, the Dutch copied this superior concept from the Frisians, not without success, calling it Gouda and Edam

cheese. It is a pity the copying took place before the patent office opened its doors. Edam and Gouda are both places in the area which was designated Frisian some thousand years ago.

Another speciality is *Fryske nageltsjetsiis*, Frisian 'clove cheese' which contains cloves and cumin. In the past it also contained herbs, which gave the cheese a greenish tint.

Culinary joys

As a people who are descended from farmers, Frisians value the amount of food over its taste, so they are more properly described as gourmands than gourmets.

"As a people descended from farmers, Frisians value the amount of food over its taste."

A heritage from the past is *potstro*. Many a Frisian adult wakes up screaming, dreaming he was forced to eat *potstro* again. *Potstro* is basically a sort of sour milk with hard pieces in it which is eaten with syrup. Laws against child abuse banned this dish from the dinner table. Not surprisingly, there are no Frisian restaurants anywhere in the world, not even in Frisia.

When historians debate how close the Old Frisians were to the Old English genetically and culturally, the hypothesis of a close relationship is strongly supported by the existence of nightmarish dishes on both sides of the North Sea: *potstro* on the Frisian side and semolina on the English side. Small wonder then that both England and Frisia have been well able to fight off foreign invaders.

The nation's much-loved confection is *oranjekoek* – a cake-like concoction (i.e. neither bread nor cake) that is flavoured with candied orange peel, aniseed and nutmeg, and glazed with icing that in bygone days may have been orange but is now rose-pink. It has an almond paste filling and is crowned with whipped cream – which is served with most cakes and desserts in Frisia.

“The name *oranjekoek* testifies to Frisian fidelity to the House of Orange... surprising until one realises that it is actually of Frisian origin.”

The name 'orange cake' testifies to Frisian fidelity to the House of Orange. This loyalty to what is now the royal house of The Netherlands may seem surprising until one realises that it is actually of Frisian origin. Yes, they lost the economic war against Holland but they won the struggle for the throne. It is the Frisians' regret that parliamentary democracy has turned the throne into what is merely a piece of furniture.

The link between Frisia and the royal house had a political motive. Both had the same all-powerful enemy: the body of merchants ruling Holland, who in modern times turned multi-national, and style themselves Shell and Unilever. It is they who really govern Holland and Frisia alike. Forget your sorrow by treating yourself to another piece of delicious *oranjekoek*.

Sense of Humour

The Frisian sense of humour specialises in slapstick. For example:

Two friends are constructing a loft together. One of them walks across the old floor not knowing that it has been constructed of a thin sheet of hardboard. The other one knows, so is flabbergasted to see his friend stand where the floor cannot possibly support him. For one second. He falls through, but manages to remain dangling by his fingers from the edge, blood running from his scratches. His mate cannot help him because he is helpless with laughter, though he manages to combine his laughs with apologies for laughing.

“Humour of the absurd is a defining characteristic of Frisian literature and may well be rooted in traditional (tall) story telling.”

Another popular form of humour is the absurd. It's a defining characteristic of Frisian literature, and may well be rooted in traditional (tall) story-telling, which is characteristic of oral cultures. The Frisian language harbours proverbs which take a surreal view of the world, predating the existentialism of Sartre and Camus by several centuries.

For instance: 'The world is rough, who functions well is tough, said the man cleaning the moat with a strainer.' Frisia is full of moats. They were used in ancient times to encircle fortified cities and manor houses and are normally cleaned out with a large rake. The image of a man cleaning the moat with a strainer is meant to ridicule not just the man but also the moral imperative of toughness and rationality itself. A truth expressed and denied at the same time.

“The Frisian language harbours proverbs which take a surreal view of the world.”

Culture

History

The Frisians consider knowledge of the past to be an essential element of their cultural heritage, probably because the present is not much to speak of.

A broadcasting company instigated a poll in which the inhabitants of the various Dutch provinces were asked questions about their regional past. The Frisians turned out to be number one.

Advocates of Frisian culture tend to resort to

historical arguments when the linguistic ones don't convince the unbeliever. It is pointed out that the name 'Frisia' is mentioned in Greek and Roman sources. Didn't Pliny describe how floating trees made Frisian waters dangerous for ships to sail in? Didn't Tacitus describe a heroic battle between Frisians and Romans because it was the first time a Germanic tribe had defeated the Roman army?

"The Frisians consider knowledge of the past to be an essential element of their cultural heritage."

In Roman days, the Frisians were confined to two of the three northern provinces. A few centuries later they appear in Old English literature, they are found southward as far as Antwerp, and northward as far as Hamburg.

By the 9th century there are Frisian streets, where Frisian merchants live, in Cologne, in Rome, in York and in Stockholm. Rome has a Frisian church dating back to this time. It's actually just around the corner from the Vatican.

According to Tacitus, the antics of the Frisians earned them a special reputation among their fellow Germanic tribes. And, as far as Frisians are concerned, they never lost it.

Painting

Local culture dictates that the window frames and doors of farms are painted in fresh white and green (though the front door may sometimes be painted brown).

As for canvas painting, mention must be made of Lawrence Alma-Tadema who emigrated in 1870 from Frisia to England where he became tremendously popular, so much so that he was knighted. His subject matter is slick, his technique accurate. His historical paintings provide an idealised picture of the elite, often the Roman elite. Soon after his death he fell from favour but the present cultural and political swing to the right has made it possible for him to recover, in part, his earlier fame.

“Many people consider modern art to be garbage. Jopie Huisman took this literally. He paints it.”

But the question remains. How did a people steeped in cow dung, skates and *potstro* give rise to a Victorian aesthete?

To even the score, there is another famous painter in Frisia, Jopie Huisman. Many people consider modern art to be garbage. Jopie Huisman took this literally. He paints it. He used his not inconsiderable talent to give consequence to old shoes, clothes, a discarded broken doll, and so on. A museum in Workum is dedicated to his work. He paints much more than just garbage, and his paintings have a poignant emotional quality that is much admired. These techniques testify to the two extremes existing side by side in the complex Frisian psyche which harmonise in Huisman's paintings: things tossed away and considered worthless become things of beauty, a joy for ever.

Literature

The Frisian language owes much to Gysbert Japicx, a minor baroque poet of the 17th century who proved that work of quality could be written in the local language. This would earn him the eternal gratitude of the Frisian nation – and a statue. Forgotten for a considerable time, he was rediscovered, together with the Frisian language itself, in the Romantic age. A folk literature came into existence, bubbling over with so much life that Dickens cuts a pale figure beside it. The brothers Halbertsma were the brains behind a successful magazine publishing these folk stories and mixing them with sentimental poems (brother Eeltje) and quasi-scientific bragging about the Frisian language (brother Joost).

“A minor baroque poet of the 17th century proved that work of quality could be written in the local language.”

Brother Joost, a linguist, corresponded with all

the big shots of his day, including the Grimms who were also brothers. Joost began working on a Frisian etymological dictionary but was too lazy to get beyond the letter F, of 'Frisian', like the very nationalist he was.

Brother Eeltje, who had studied in Heidelberg (Germany), brought home a beer-drinking song, wrote a new text to it, and that is how the Frisian anthem was born. The first line runs: 'Frisian blood, flow upward, bubble and foam, and race through our veins.' Somehow one gets the impression that the beer consumed in Germany was still bubbling, foaming and racing through Eeltje's brain when he composed this song.

A modern day great Frisian literary figure, and winner of the prestigious Gysbert Japicx prize, Tsjêbbe Hettinga was a poet whose work celebrates 'the sea, the sky, the seagulls, the cattle, the grass, but most of all the shore, the line where two worlds meet.'

An admirer of Dylan Thomas, Hettinga's poems are described as being about: 'great romantic themes, such as love, decay and death, the longing for strange shores and the longing to be back home. It is not a poetry of fine-spun reasoning but one of images. The images [he] evokes seem to be prompted by the sound patterns of the Frisian language...'

Here is an extract from *Wounded continents*:

From the clacking wooden shoes to the snuffling
cows
The milkmaid bouncing along in the back
[of the cart] has
A touch of summer – and her fingers – forever
In her hair, as blond as straw kissed by the moon.

Frisia's most experimental writer, Trinus Riemersma, writes bitter books mixing three or more plots in the best post-modernist tradition. His works nevertheless remain readable because of their exaggerated comedy. Frisian detective fiction similarly testifies to a lively sense of humour which is singularly lacking in the earnest counterparts from the Nordic or English-speaking world.

Nowadays there are even experimental novels written in Frisian, which few are keen to read. If Frisian dies out again as a written language, as in the Renaissance, no doubt the experimental novel will be responsible for it.

Newspapers

Reading the newspaper is another leisure activity, especially for the elderly. Supposedly they want to be 'informed'. However the two main Frisian newspapers present a mix of local news (i.e. gossip) and self-congratulatory opinions. There is the *Friesch Dagblad* for the puritans, and the *Leeuwarder*

Courant for the socialists. As both come close to being instruments for political propaganda, it's tough luck for those of a different persuasion.

The newspapers have managed to solve the problem of writing correct Frisian. They are 95% written in Dutch, thereby reducing the number of language mistakes by 95%. Frisian words are occasionally slipped into the headlines, in the form of quotations and jokes on puns, which is probably some sort of subconscious indoctrination. The good news is that the number of Frisian words in the newspapers is going up by roughly half a percent every year: in two centuries there will be a newspaper in Frisian again.

“The newspapers have managed to solve the problem of writing correct Frisian. They are 95% written in Dutch.”

Quirks of the Language

The 19th-century Frisian linguist Joost Halbertsma had his defence ready when haughty Dutchmen ridiculed Frisian as a silly farmers' language. He pointed out that Frisian was sweet to the ears, since it had a number of sounds in common with French, which were lacking in Dutch.

For example, the Frisian word '*moarns*' (in the

morning) reproduces the vowel that makes the second syllable of 'Françoise' so attractive.

If this were not enough, he pointed out the kinship between Frisian and that other noble language, English, as evidenced by the initial sound in words like '*tsiis*' (cheese, Dutch '*kaas*') and '*tsjerke*' (church, Dutch '*kerk*') as in this ancient rhyme:

English: 'Butter, bread, and green cheese is good English and good Fries.'

Frisian: '*Bûter, brea, en griene tsiis is goed Ingelsk en goed Fries.*'

On the whole, Frisian and English prefer palatable pronunciations, with words being pronounced in the front of the mouth. Dutch and German settle for unpalatable guttural pronunciations. Take a word like *swiet*, which the English pronounce like the Frisians with a vowel in the front of the mouth: sweet. The Dutch pronounce it as *zoet*, with an ominous vowel pronounced in the back of the mouth, rhyming with the English word 'soot'.

The following words and expressions reveal something of the philosophic genius of the Frisian nation:

'*In goeie jonge*' – 'A good boy', but the actual meaning is 'A harmless, mediocre figure'. The link between the concepts of harmlessness and mediocrity may well hark back to the medieval period of civil wars and anarchy.

'Net sa best' – 'Not so very good.' In reality 'a disaster'. The Frisians alternately employ hyperbole and understatement. Understatement is generally used where hyperbole would be felt as giving a too realistic description of the situation.

'It koe minder' – 'It could be worse.' Typically used by lottery-winners. Another example of Frisian understatement.

'Dat sil 't wol' – 'That seems to be true'. Actually 'I do not believe a word of what you're telling me.'

'Moat dat no sa?' – 'Does it have to be like that?' An expression of strong disapproval.

The words *glûpende, bare, ferskriklike, ûnhuere, tige, ûntyglike, seldsume, mâle, rare, allemachtige, alderraarste, allerferskuorrendste,* and more, all mean 'very' – proof, if proof were needed, of the Frisian love of aggrandizement. These words are used interchangeably and so often by Frisians that the European Community interpreters would have stopped interpreting them, if only Frisian had been a permissible language in EU deliberations.

But the language has something to celebrate. Frisian is now available in Google Translate.

The Author

Eric Hoekstra was born in 1960 in that special part of The Netherlands called Frisia. As a pure Dutchman, he worked in Amsterdam, before, as a pure Frisian, he moved to Leeuwarden to work for the Frisian Academy, a research institute that studies the Frisian language, culture and history. It also promotes interest in other minority cultures like the Welsh, the Scots and the Catalans. The most popular are probably the Scots, if only because they produce outstanding pop groups and have an accent that is pleasant to Frisian ears. And they are almost independent.

What with the upsurge of nationalism everywhere in Europe, he is all in favour of the rest of The Netherlands finally becoming independent of Frisia. Provided there are no costs involved. For Frisia.

List of titles in the Xenophobe's® Guides series

Xenophobe's® guides

Available as printed books and e-books:

The Albanians
The Americans
The Aussies
The Austrians
The Belgians
The Canadians
The Chinese
The Czechs
The Danes
The Dutch
The English
The Estonians
The Finns
The French
The Frisians
The Germans
The Greeks
The Icelanders
The Irish
The Israelis
The Italians
The Japanese
The Kiwis
The Norwegians
The Poles
The Portuguese
The Russians
The Scots
The Spanish
The Swedes
The Swiss
The Welsh

Xenophobe's® lingo learners

French
German
Greek
Italian
Spanish

Xenophobe's Guides